I PROMISE I STILL LOVE YOU

ASSIA MESSAOUDI

I PROMISE I STILL LOVE YOU

A Collection of Poems

Laura,

Thank you for always being a shining ray of light in my life. I'm glad to have you.

Love,
- Assia M.

ASSIA MESSAOUDI

Life Rattle Press
New Publishers Series
Toronto, Canada

Published by Life Rattle New Writers Series
Life Rattle Press
196 Crawford Street
Toronto, Ontario, Canada
M6J 2V6

Cover design by Jasmine Noseworthy Persaud
Typeset by Sophia Luo
Copy edited by Lee Parpart
Illustrations by Lina Mobeireek and Reema Mobeireek

Library and Archives Canada Cataloguing in Publication

Messaoudi, Assia, 1995-, author.
I Promise I Still Love You / Assia Messaoudi.

Poems.
ISBN 978-1-987936-61-2
This is an original print edition of I Promise I Still Love You.
Set in Sabon

For the women we used to be,
the women we still are, and the
women we're trying to become.

ACKNOWLEDGMENTS

Thank you to every woman who has told me her story. I hope I do you justice. You are beautiful and brave in the way you continue to exist.

Thank you to mama for being the woman I hope to become and for loving your daughters unconditionally. You've taught me about strength and perseverance and you've sacrificed so much for me. This is for you. I love you.

Thank you to friends, family, and strangers for believing enough in my work to invest in it. Thank you for reading these poems. I hope you find yourselves in happy parts, and that even if you don't, this inspires healing.

Thank you to Jasmine for creating everything I envisioned. You, and my cover, are more beautiful than I could ever have imagined.

Thank you to Lee Parpart, my copy editor, for understanding my thought processes and fine-tuning everything. Thank you for your encouragement and support and accepting the additional pages I provided you with; it means the world.

Thank you to Sophia for piecing everything together.

Thank you to Zaynab and Nancie for being part of my book and part of my experience. Your words have helped me in more ways than you could ever imagine. Thank you for spring cleanings both in my house and in my mind. Thank you for the long phone calls and for always being there when I spiralled; I love you.

Thank you to Lina and Reema for creating such beautiful art in these pages. Thank you for giving me hope in my darkest times and continuing to be rays of light for me. I love you.

Thank you to Lindsay for trusting me and understanding me in ways no one else ever could. You're the one person I talk to every day and I wouldn't change that for anything. I love you.

Thank you Khadija for always listening—to these poems, to my story, and to the person I am now. You have always been everything.

Thank you Erin for both believing me and believing in me. Thank you for being my badass pixie dream girl. I love you.

Thank you to Addie for being beautiful and compassionate. Thank you for helping me with every nitpicky part of this process. You are a godsend and I love you.

Thank you to Jay for the daily music that drove me to write more. Thank you for being there to help talk me through this process. Thank you for showcasing my words in your own book. I value you.

Thank you to Florence and Angela for constant reassurance and validation. Thank you for keeping me up to speed. I couldn't have done this without you.

Thank you to Zayneb for always understanding where I come from, I love you.

Thank you to everyone at Life Rattle Press for taking a chance on me; I hope to make you as proud as I am to have published a book with you.

Thank you to Guy Allen for believing in 18-year-old Assia four years ago and 22-year-old Assia today. You are what made me want to pursue an undergrad in Professional Writing. You worked with me to make this book possible and always encouraged my success. I am eternally grateful.

Thank you to the writers who gave permission to have their work appear alongside my own. Ocean Vuong, Salma Deera, Taylor Jenkins Reid, it is an honour and a blessing to have three of my biggest inspirations be part of something I created.

Thank you to poets like Warsan Shire, Yasmin Z, Clementine von Radics, Karys Peterson-Katz, and Lucas Regazzi, whose work influenced a lot of my own. Your words have been a constant source of inspiration for me.

Thank you to all the members of poetry circle for having open ears, open minds, and open hearts. Thank you for compliments and constructive criticism alike. I am grateful for your words and vulnerability. Thank you to Brent Wood for your faith in me.

Thank you to my circus troupe for making sure I always had chalk on my palms every time I felt myself slipping during this process.

Thank you to everyone in my life who has supported or inspired me in some way, shape, or form over the years. Whether you are still part of my life or not, I love you endlessly and effortlessly.

CONTENTS

STAGE 1: LEARNING

STAGE II: LOVING

STAGE III: BREAKING

STAGE IV: LEAVING

Who would believe us
now? My voice cracking
like bones inside the radio.
Silly me. I thought love was real
& the body imaginary.
— Ocean Vuong, "Eurydice"

STAGE 1: LEARNING

"That's what you do when you want something.
You don't look for reasons why it won't work.
You look for reasons why it will."
—Taylor Jenkins Reid, *Maybe in Another Life*

I think I knew who you were from the beginning. I *know* I knew who you were. I found my journal from the month we met, and all I wrote was "he's going to destroy me." I found my poems from when we first started talking, and none of them sound happy. It makes me feel stupid, now that the fog has cleared from my eyes and you don't look beautiful anymore. I feel stupid for thinking that the way we were when we were together was normal. I feel stupid for believing you didn't realize that I was in love with you. I know now, you knew everything, and pretending you didn't was part of the manipulation. You wanted me to puzzle over every glance from you, and second-guess every change in your tone. You enjoyed watching me struggle.

When we first met, you'd suffered a terrible loss. I felt sorry for you. I pitied you for the shocking way she—the woman you loved before me—left your life. That pity turned into love, and that love turned into fear, and that fear turned into hate, and that hate turned me into someone else. Our foundation was mutual pain, mutual illness, and mutual loss. Despite knowing that misery loves company, I should have been more careful with the company I kept.

marigold

it's been days since i first sat beside you
you went through so many cigarettes
i thought they were smoke signals
i didn't know whether or not to send help

i kept trying to lighten the mood
even when you laughed
it looked like there was something missing
i finally understand what it means when
people say your smile doesn't reach your eyes

you keep having conversations with ghosts
they never talk back
that doesn't stop you
from becoming one of them

you make telephones out of tin cans and string
just to hear her voice on the other end
when it's silent, you start to think
maybe those things never worked anyway

remember when you used to chase after sunsets
now you chase down drinks
like you can see her face at the bottom of your cup
the burn in your throat tastes like her
and you can't let go of it
you wake with a hangover that feels like her voice
throbbing against your temple
telling you to go fuck yourself

you look into the mirror like you're looking at
damaged goods
like someone flipped over the shipping box
ignoring the warnings plastered on the outside
i want to tell you i get it
i fall in love with damaged goods
i see the good before i see what's damaged

you tell me you stopped going to church
that the only time you spoke to god was in bed
the only time you saw god was when you looked at her
the only time you heard god was when
she whispered in your ear and
oh god, this is too much

i know no one will ever know how she looked
when she walked in front of you
i know you feel lucky to have had the privilege
of witnessing her chest rising and falling with every breath
you're jealous of god because she promised you forever
but now he gets to keep her close
so you write poems instead of sleeping
and i never thought angels could cry until i met you

you said you've never been much of a musician
so why does your voice sound like a song
i fell in love as the sun set over the horizon
illuminating your face with the colour of marigold
and i can't look away

when i saw you i saw a phoenix
you heal everyone around you only to combust
but still you climb out of the ashes

i know you don't like it when people live through your poetry
but i hope you see yourself in mine
and i hope it makes you sing
until your voice breaks
and your pain shatters
and the sun starts shining at midnight
then somehow for the first time in two years
you feel your eyelids flutter shut

i hope you find a love that lets you sleep early and sleep in
a love that makes you leave the door unlocked
and the windows open
a love that feels like home
after you've spent your whole life moving

infatuated

don't ask me if i dream of you
all i ever do is dream
not of you but of everything you do
midnight drives and bloodshot eyes
fill my subconscious like a glass of water
that's so busy being half full
we never notice it starting to overflow
what does it mean when days feel like weeks with you
and yet no amount of time is ever enough
is it okay to write love poems when you're not in love?
is it okay to look at you like i do?
i just don't know what this is
and for the first time ever that's okay
who cares if we're not fucking
if our hearts keep touching this way
who cares if i'll probably hate you tomorrow
i still love you today
and that can feel like being buried alive
don't blame me if my body still starts to decay
but if the flowers start to bloom from the dirt then
i blame you
because you showed me
that good things can still grow from tainted soil
not every word that leaves your mouth
tears apart my skin
like before
we have matured like fine wine
but neither of us wants to take a sip
neither of us wants to take the risk
i don't want to overdrink
and lose my inhibitions
say something i'll regret
that's why these days
i stick to dreaming

we break like porcelain

there's a dark cloud raining over your head
you leave your umbrella locked in your car
along with the key
we break in and you look over your shoulder
as if we're doing something wrong
when we drive
you keep your hand on the gear
always ready to slip into reverse

you talk about how you give yourself away
like you're not made up of one-armed hugs
and missed texts and calls
and never letting anyone see you cry

you see, this isn't pity
i tried to wrap my head around you
and it kept snapping back into place
you came up to me with a neon sign flashing
"welcome home" and "do not enter"
and they're still coursing over each other
i have one foot in and one foot out
both feet are facing you

i don't need to know the bad parts
i don't need to meet the skeletons
that slam against your closet door
you let them out and they share your bed now
that's probably why you can't sleep

we're nothing but ruins
due to the ones who've ruined us
we are rome after its fall
we had an empire
but now all we do is talk about what used to be
we try to pick up the pieces
and the glass cuts our fingers
we're left for dead in the midst of it
the remnants look too much like pieces of us

it's no wonder we see our reflections
you're sitting right in front of me
with your body turned like you're going to leave
i'm fighting for your attention
all i do is beg and plead
and forget to say please
i think that being mean will put your mind at ease
because you think when i'm being cruel
i'll say what i mean
and mean what i say
i don't even know if this means anything

i know it's hard for you to look at me
but i have to say
i'll take the pain
i'll take the angst
i'll take what i can get

i'll swallow my pride
and maybe i'll choke
but i'll have a few chugs of
whatever you're having to keep it down
i'm nothing more to you than second-hand smoke
you get the damage without the rush
you're left with nothing but blackened lungs

you're not standing in front of moving vehicles
but still you're the one who gets crushed
you look at me like i'm a crutch
but sweetheart, your legs were never broken
you were just making an excuse not to walk away

if losing you is the saddest thing i'll ever do then
i'm choosing grief
i'm choosing car crashes and burnt metal
and the smell of your skin
at two in the morning
when you stumble in drunk off of the love of someone else
i'm choosing an addict who got addicted to the feeling
instead of the drug

you swallow pills marked "love"
they lodge in your throat
i give you the heimlich maneuver
and you spit out poetry each time
it spills onto the porcelain bathtub
i'll read it with a vengeance
but i don't mean to pry
it's just that i'm scared
it's been a while since i've cried
i think i'm losing whatever feelings i used to have inside
i'll make your bed while you make up your mind
you'll start packing your bags
and i'll try to buy myself time
i'll cruise down memory lane until
you remember i can't drive
you'll say you never cared
i'll love it when you lie

but i'll be a pit stop to wherever you're going
i'll understand if you leave me behind
you don't take hostels with you
hostels are the people whose names you forget
they're a momentary place to catch up on missed sleep
i want to tell you it's okay if you decide
you want to wake up
it's okay if you keep driving

mtl

i keep mistaking the drops of rain on my window for your tears
though you're not even here
it keeps storming over montreal
but the day still ends with a sunset
more beautiful than the city itself
the glow sears my retinas
i welcome the slow burn
that results in showers pouring down my cheeks
i keep thinking that our future looks bleak
i've been climbing mountains for the past two weeks
pretending i could see the toronto skyline
if i tilt my head just right
the same way i can see you laughing
if i close my eyes tight
you have not laughed for a while
and missing something like
our city, or your laugh,
makes me want to create mirages
where someone else has memories
i am making seats out of sidewalks
i am forcing myself into cracks where i don't belong
and it almost fits
sort of, at least
you're not telling me to get the fuck up
and i'm not telling you that
i am nothing but a foreigner to this town
and to your heart
i can't seem to get the hang of the language
so i roll my tongue and purse my mouth just right but
i don't remember how to ask for directions in french
and the one thing i want to do is go to you
all i know how to say is
je t'aime
but i can't tell that to the bus driver
and hope your ears perk up
and hope that somehow you show up
to my house at half past midnight because
cherry blossoms are blooming everywhere right now

except inside of us
and for some indiscernible reason you missed my voice
and the way i laugh at my own jokes
when i'm afraid nobody else will
i want that classic movie thing
where the credits never roll
because it never seems to end
but my life keeps being advertised as a romantic tragedy
that's kind of what we are, romantic
but still tragic
we only build ourselves up so
it will hurt more when we tear each other down
and i don't know when the bustle of the city
started to feel like a ghost town
or when drive-by shootings became as common
as you driving to my place but
never letting me know you're outside
i don't want to admit i look for your headlights
out my window
when i try to whisper
your name and it comes out like a
scream that echoes
through the hollow walls of this house
and everyone is sleeping except us
you pretend not to hear my heart
trying to claw its way out of my chest
and rush to yours like a highway collision
i don't care about the damage
but every moment i spend with you
i have to stop myself from calling an ambulance
in case both of us combust
i don't want anything from you
i just want any thing from you
i'll take whatever you're willing to give me
i keep waiting for you to turn this casual dinner into a date
this coincidence into fate
this friendship into a ship
that you don't try to sink
no matter how much your mind tells you to
with us, you don't have to overthink

it's just
when i come back
i want to go home
and i hope your eyes will still shine for me like a porch light
and the door to your heart swings open
see, even though i've been gone a while
i don't want to go anywhere else without you
so if you want, please let me in—
i promise i'm not leaving anytime soon

l.o.v.e

you always stand to talk to me
with one foot facing the opposite direction
you're always gone before you even start making conversation
and i pretend not to notice your eyes locked on someone else
while mine search your mouth
for the stories you string together like screenplays
and everything is so vivid
and i can imagine every word because
they repeat themselves in pictures that burn
the back of my eyelids for the next goddamn month

i taught myself how to read people but i stop after the prologue
it hurts too much to flip the pages
i know it's not fiction

people keep telling me i talk too much about love
but we always want to talk about a backstabbing bitch
pretend this is a dinner party and love is a person
i will tell you this:

love drew me in under a false premise
love disguised itself as something else
we went along with it
romanticizing cupid as if there's something beautiful
about somebody shooting arrows into your heart
so how can i fall in love when i know what it does?

love is the forgotten word that hides on the tip of my tongue
i only remember it at three a.m. next week
by the time i figure it out, i am already too late

calm before the storm

last night i searched a list of the most
beautiful words in the english language
i kept looking for your name
it keeps beating against the frontal lobe of my brain
the area that's supposed to make good decisions
but somehow keeps choosing you
then again the frontal lobe doesn't develop
until you're twenty-five
or is it twenty-two
i can't seem to decide
all i do is lurch between
giving myself to somebody and getting hurt
and someone forgot to tell me that they're the same things

i'm writing your name in my journal
i never even had a journal until i met you
okay—i did. i just never used it
you look like the kind of person who keeps a journal
and drinks scotch
maybe explains why you're sticking to me
you're my optical illusion
every time i blink you disappear and i have to figure you out
again

i just don't know
how to let go of people
i just met you, and you know me better than
anyone else
better than myself
better than those standardized tests
that make you think back to the last time you had a good night's
rest
you wear your insecurities like a wardrobe
i just want to watch you get undressed

maybe i'm just crazy

but i keep memorizing the way

you move your hands when you speak
the way you drive like you have nowhere to be
the way you chain smoke behind a laugh
that you don't want me to see
i always had trouble writing long poetry before you met me
now look at me, stringing together words like i have so much to say

look at me go
i'm a one-woman show
i'll take my pain and your pain
and turn it into something beautiful
so someone can come along and romanticize
this generation of broken souls
i'm just full of clichés
and i want to write about how you simply take my breath away
you seem like someone that i would meet once in a lifetime
and i know every word you say translates to you begging me to stay away
but i always take one step closer to the flames
and you open your arms to welcome me
even though we both know you're going to destroy me
one of these days

i always thought about the phrase till death do us part
and i thought it made sense
but you don't even let death stop you from
putting paper to pen

you make me want to call my preschool exes
and ask where they went
i'm such a shopaholic
look at all the love that i've spent

i guess i fetishize this pain because
it hurts too much to say
that i can be whatever you need
if you just decide to stay

i know you're a walking contradiction

because you say you don't care but i keep seeing you cry
over people who you love
and your whole life passing you by
i know what it's like to live like any second you're gonna die
i know what it's like to dig your grave while you're still alive
and the kids around you play with toys
because they still have lots of time
even though time is a construct i still look at clocks
but somehow when i'm with you
it doesn't feel like time i've lost
i guess i just want to say
i hope nothing gets in the way
of someone saying "i understand you"
just by saying your name

voicemail

hello?
are you there?
i could use a distraction right now
your voice is the only thing that works
i can't help it
i'm drawn to you like a bull is drawn to red in the ring
i'm charging
i can't see anything but that colour
i know it's going to hurt
when my body finally connects with yours but
things are kind of tough right now
my life is a jigsaw puzzle i can't solve
because some of the pieces are missing
and you're the only one who gets it
i'm tied down to train tracks and my body can't seem to move
i'm also the oncoming train
i'm steering the vehicle of my destruction
my throat feels like it's on fire but no screams ever come out
i feel like i overdosed on prozac
before knowing that it isn't supposed to make you happy
that it's just supposed to make you stop living like a ghost
but nothing brings back the dead
not alcohol, not antidepressants
not poetry, not flowers
not books full of words you wish you'd said
i know you'll hate me for saying this but
you make me feel a bit more alive
like trying on clothes and finally finding the right size
but with you it's like finding a home
with cracks that you call character
and no one really gets why you don't just find another place
how do you tell them your bed
would feel different somewhere else
how do you tell them you wouldn't be able to fall asleep
things aren't great right now
but you're the only one who makes them a little less painful

insomniac

i tattooed your heartbeat into my skin
so that even when your heart stops
it'll somehow still exist
and i wanted to tell you that i stopped sleeping
so i wouldn't have to dream about you
but you started showing up
in my insomnia-induced hallucinations
laughing and talking about stupid shit
and it kind of drove me crazy
because i couldn't move my mouth to tell you
my tongue aches
with the muted taste of everything
except yours
i just want to kiss you like
a bottle connecting with a lakeside rock
i think i'll shatter upon impact
but i'll survive
i don't mind if you decide not to pick up the mess
if you choose instead to lay down to rest
i promise i'll hold you close enough to feel
your own heartbeat on my chest

parkdale

you remind me of
the broken lights in my bedroom that refuse to be fixed
they keep resisting every press of the switch
keep flickering until they die out completely
the electric bill stays the same
my landlord tells me i'm wasting my energy
trying to fix these broken bulbs
but they keep flashing as if they're begging me to do something
from dusk to dawn
when they're supposed to stay on
i wait for them to stop wailing at me like police sirens
this isn't an emergency but your eyes say otherwise
my eyes shift to where
my fingers are folded in my lap
you have a cigarette in one hand and a drink in the other
talking to me about past dreams
telling me that these days they're dead
maybe you should've never put that dream catcher
over your head on your childhood bed
because it only gave you nightmares
the ones you have when your mom forgets to tuck you in at
night
you look sad when you tell me i smile at you just like she did
it's not quite pity
but she looks at you like you're going to disappear any second
checking for a pulse like she's checking her watch
reminding you that your heart has a curfew
offering you free rent because she keeps trying to buy you more
time
maybe it's because
you look like a suicide attempt
all desperation and could've been
carving lines into your skin
as if to make roads for yourself to walk on
do you mind if i ask you where you've been?
you're built to swallow sandpaper
it makes the smoke go down more smoothly
and i keep brushing the cigarette ash from between your dimples

because craters should be hollow
and the moon controls the tide
so slow your single tear for a second, sweetheart
stretch it out
let it really hit you
like when you slap someone across the face
you're only trying to recreate the waves
connecting with the shoreline
it's almost violent
i think that's why the red sea tastes like rust
every poem spills out of your mouth like a sweet jack and ginger
you drink your worries out of a cracked mason jar
i just want to borrow your burden and carry it for a little bit
just until you get the hang of it
i'll rub the tension from your shoulders
it's too tough to carry people's expectations
when all the bridges you didn't want to burn started breaking
you sell your love in thrift stores
with a sign flashing "used"
or "feels like new"
or "wash gently"
because the fabric shrinks or stretches
so you keep replacing your wardrobe
you wear past lovers like tattoos
permanently branded onto your skin
it's the first thing people notice when they look at you
they keep asking
were you ever in love?
but they mean to say
please fall in love with me
because you look like the kind of person who loves easily
you look like someone who kisses like they mean it
who holds you in a way that says
i'm not going anywhere, even with one foot out the door
and maybe you could be that person, but
you don't tell anyone
that sometimes your heart feels too heavy for your body
sometimes it weighs you down
because each beat of your heart sounds like
the ticking of the clock reminding you there's not much time left

to fall in love or be remembered
so you fall in love with everyone
you speak to them in tongues
and they answer you in the same language
they're not able to forget you
morning comes and they search for your body
on the other side of the bed
morning comes and they search for letters left on the dresser
morning comes and they hope last night meant something
morning comes and they kiss their phone numbers into your skin
breathing love into your open mouth
you don't tell anyone though
that these lovers all taste the same
like extra sweet jack and gingers:
somehow, too good to be true

lcbo

my tipsy tongue can't pronounce your name
it's all jumbled, it streams out of my mouth
and splashes on the floor and against the walls
40% vodka makes me 100% in love with you
and i want to say it
but it comes out in waterfalls escaping my lips
i'm not making any sense
and i'm slurring my syllables
as you sit across from me throwing your head back to laugh
because you've never seen me this happy before
i want to tell you
i promise it's not just the alcohol
i wouldn't want to be with anyone else
instead i stumble into your arms
you steady me with a smile
and somehow that says more than words ever could

xo

i want to kiss you
the way a car kisses a tree
but i don't want to call it an accident
i didn't fall asleep at the wheel
or drink before i drove
i just wanted to see what would happen
find out if your body would reject mine
there's still yellow caution tape around your heart from last time
but you haven't yet outlined your body with chalk
so maybe we could talk
for a little
about your commitment issues
i get you on that
i spend more time thinking about committing suicide
than committing to the person i'm loving
we're an ugly kind of fucked up
the kind that even the best poets
can't write about
we're so messed up
even the illusion of beauty
can't save us

if john green met you he'd have another bestseller

this is the second sleepless night i've had
in which you left me second-guessing
every statement that leaves your mouth
sounds too much like a question
and tonight i'm confused
my pillow smells like you
my blanket feels like you
and the floor i'm splayed against
holds me rigidly
like you
i'm trying to make sense of your actions
i'm trying to give you my two cents
and tell you hey
why do you talk like you're the protagonist
in a young adult novel
like your only goal is to make the reader fall in love with you
i should've never picked up the book but your eyes scream
"read"
and it startled me into
taking the guard off my emergency lighter
so i could burn the damn pages
i don't know if i should find out what happens next
because i was never a fan of unhappy endings
i have too much personal experience with that
and i just wanted to live in a fantasy for a little bit
but i spent too much time playing with matches
and one foot hanging out the door until i learned that
indecision smells like burned flesh
and burned-out human beings look like empty fuel tanks
always running low
and i know what that's like
but sleeping just isn't an option
when every bed feels like a pavement
and every person feels like a gas chamber
your bad back has you suffocating
and i love you like fourth of july fireworks
like false independence
we keep paying the price for choosing to be free

because you want it all and i want all of you
and you're asleep right now
thinking about everything but me
but i'm awake trying so hard to figure you out
i just want to be enough
so kiss me
like an abandoned house just went up in flames
like a split second of excitement
before we get back to the mundane
kiss me like you'd choose me
without a gun pressed to your head
kiss me like my body isn't shaped like the bullet
in a game of russian roulette
just do it, baby
please
i don't even care if all we're doing is
playing make-believe

small

i hope you haven't noticed me
clinging to your coattails
gazing at you nervously
i trace your name into my hands
i long for you like a drowning woman
longs for air
i always choke on salt water instead
once you save me from the current
we walk to the corner store and i buy a lighter
so i can look at that
instead of the fire in your eyes
and a can of arizona hoping it will chase down
the bitterness of the things you tell me
i wanted you to know that
if my fingers shake when i'm near you
it's not my low blood sugar
i'm working up the courage not to touch you until i leave
okay it's my blood sugar
but still i'm working up the courage to keep
my hands to myself
my mind to myself
i'm trying to keep these feelings to myself
leaves start falling in springtime to beat you to your death
nature destroys itself
the willows and i have wept
and it is beautiful to see the sunset take its time with you
i can't stay out as long
i can't take my time
my curfew cures few
it's a malady that leaves you waiting in my driveway
till morning comes
and it leaves my mother anxious by the door
until i get home
she sniffs out your scent like a hound on the prowl
says she's trying to keep me from getting my heart broken
but mother,
what's another crack on something that's already been shattered?
i keep waiting for you to turn into a life lesson

i know what i'm doing
i know how to deal with pain
it's something that i'm good at
i know what it's like to not find my name on a keychain
i keep looking anyway
i know what it's like to look through old conversations
you had with someone who loved you
past lovers turn into people who kiss you out of spite
i've seen the people i love destroy themselves right in front of me
and i did nothing to stop it
free will is a bitch sometimes
so was i
but i don't want to make those mistakes again
i will wait with you in a hospital room if you need me to
and i will be sitting there even if you don't
i'll check your body for a pulse while you sleep
i'll keep an extra umbrella stowed away for you in my bag
i'll buy things in doubles
i'll write you post-it notes and letters
i'll love you until you don't want me to anymore
but even when you tell me to stop
don't ask me why i still look at you the way i do
my heart is nothing but an elastic
and you're the only thing that stops it
from snapping in two

menthols

there's something ethereal about the way you light a cigarette
each flicker of fire between your fingertips
is another year shaved off your life
but i'm mesmerized anyway
you know this
i tell you i love you
until it breaks me open
and you pretend not to hear me over the car's quiet engine
and i can see myself in the road signs
on the almost empty side roads
something you'll attend to but soon forget
i say your name like my throat is about to catch fire
rushed, fumbling, guttural
you hand me a cup of hot coffee and i tell you that
your name wrecks my anatomy
you drive me to the nearest walk-in clinic and wait outside
i admit i loved you till i broke every bone in my hand
every touch caused me to splinter
now you have my marrow under your skin
spreading out like ink
and i'm apologizing the whole way home
you're pretending i have nothing important to say
so i keep repeating your name until it becomes a whisper
until it doesn't hurt so much anymore
my throat becomes an echo
and you still won't look at me
you act like you can't see
that they lied when they said love
makes you feel alive again
so is this not love
if i can feel myself dying?

STAGE II: LOVING

"Loving you was a destructive type of selfish.
It's the feeling of getting on a rollercoaster
with a faulty belt and hoping that gravity
will keep you in your seat."
—Nancie Jona

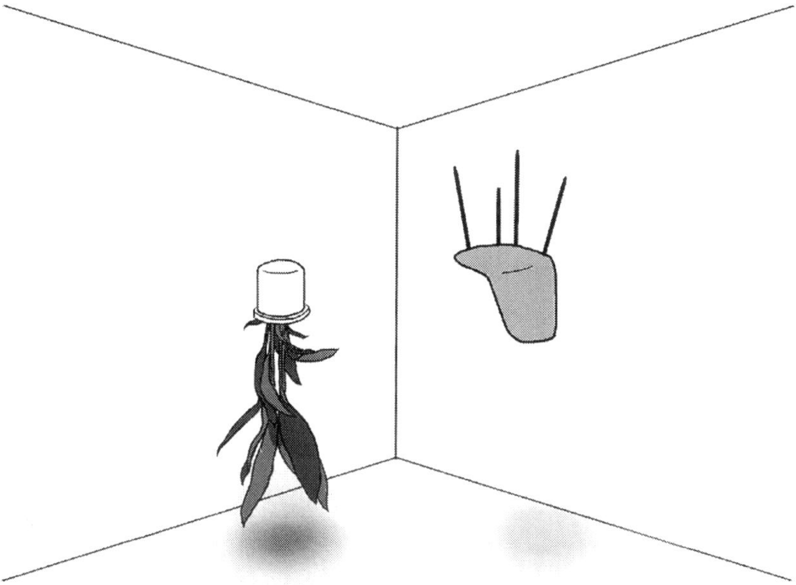

The first time you say you love me, we're in a bar in a city that isn't home. I can't touch my dinner and you can't touch me. You tell me you'll do anything to make me happy, but that you don't love me the same way. I lie and say I'm okay with that, that I'll have you in whatever way you'll let me. I sleep in your arms for the first time ever that night. You hold me. Nothing more, nothing less.

Days later, our bodies lie in the same position. You lie and say that you really want to kiss me right now, and I tell you to do it.

I mistake the static shock for electricity and say, what happened to not seeing me like that? Like a viable option?

You say that something changed.

I wish I realized that meant the only thing about to change was me.

sofa bed

send my love to the boy who dances between sweet nothings
like he's walking on eggshells
whose name rolls off my tongue like crest toothpaste
who told me he loved me while i was lying on his chest
at three in the morning with half his body already out of bed
he stayed anyway
because he sleeps better with his hands on my skin
so i tell him
the other night when you were looking into my eyes
i realized you're like a lighthouse
no matter how foggy it gets you're the one thing i can see
and i know i kiss you like a cliché
when i try to lace my tongue with your heart
and i know you notice when i kiss your neck to check for a pulse
i'm just a little scared because you live on missed deadlines
but i'm hoping that you'll ask me for an extension
hoping you'll forget that we're living on borrowed time
because you're too entranced by the way i trip over myself
and onto you
until i'm nothing more than a pair of scraped knees
throwing my head back to laugh at your shocked expression
i'm a bruised hipbone away from telling you
how much i want to hold your hand
when i think nobody's watching
and even when i know somebody is
so just
kiss me like time is frozen
like all the clocks are broken
and there's nothing but this moment
kiss me like my rent isn't already overdue
like there isn't someone else wide awake in the next room
like we're more than just two fools with better things to do
kiss me like
deadlines don't exist
like you're not walking on eggshells
like they're not scraping the soles of your feet
while i figure out how to write you a love letter
that doesn't look like a receipt

because this thing that we have is more than enough
so every time i trip over you
don't forget to help me up

fruit loops

i am painfully aware that caskets aren't made for two
but i forget that every time you take me
six feet under with you
these tears drown me with vigour
and my head is too big for my body
and your pulse is too loud for your ears
and maybe that's why you're ready to turn it off
maybe the buzzing isn't tinnitus but her voice
thrumming through your skull at a million miles an hour
telling you she misses you
maybe that's why you don't want to stay
you spent so many nights with your foot dangling off my bed
that you dreamt up a nonexistent monster
and now he lives in your chest
we share the same name
you see him every time i kiss you
and try to love your sadness away
i keep thinking that
i don't know if you'll make it to summer
but please be with me at my wedding
as my best friend or my lover
please let me believe that we're somehow enough for each other
don't make me hide pill bottles under the covers
i can't stop feeling guilty for holding onto you
because if you let yourself believe it,
this apartment was really made for two
i see myself eating dinner across the table from an invisible lover
i see myself breaking like coloured cereal bowls
i see myself dancing to your favourite song,
alone

mini me

i think our child would have your eyes
my mouth
your lopsided smile
my skin
your beauty marks
the gold in my hair
the texture of yours
my nose
your laugh
my voice
your toes
my cancer
your irregular heartbeat
our late night hospital visits
your nightmares
my insomnia
our child will have a tornado for a throat
hacking out debris
and i'll always feel selfish
for wanting my child to look like me

dear god, please break your stopwatch or stop watching us

you have an hourglass figure
grains spill from your mouth
to remind you how
little time is left
our silence fills the room
and the burden
of your impending demise
weighs on us
like a grandfather clock
every hourly bell toll
deafens you
leaves you picking seconds off the floor
and plucking them in your mouth
they cut your cheeks
like broken glass
as time tumbles from your lips
and your hourglass body
fills with quicksand

vinyl

tattoos are your attempt at sheet music
eighth notes seep out of the ink
and into your bloodstream
they're playing your favourite song
you can't recognize your own face
so you scratch it onto your body
with the needle of the record player
until you taste the melody in your mouth
until you feel closer to the music
until it becomes real
baby blue lies under your tongue
and the curve of the treble clef
invokes a past lover
you trace it until nostalgia rings in your ears
and smoke clouds your vision
and you can't see the record player anymore
but you can almost touch the music
it pricks your skin,
begging to be let in
nothing ever felt this good unless it was a sin
so you drown it in a bottle of gin
and absinth makes the heart grow fonder
and yours beats
with the baseline
until you can't help but think
that records break just as easily as people
and the fragility of the disc
echoes the way your
bones don't quite fit
your body
so you cover your sheet music
with long sleeves
add rests instead of beats
afraid that somebody will play you off key
but you are more than sheet music
you are vinyl
final
the destination and answer to every song ever played

valentine's day

maybe you stopped making my name
out of the letters in your alphabet soup
and you flinch whenever i breathe love into your ear
but i am still here
i wake up beside you almost every morning
you pull me towards you, half asleep
and talk to me in hurricanes
the things you say destroy me sometimes
i keep leaving candy hearts in your lunch box
that read "be mine" in block letters
you force them down your throat even though you hate the taste
i know you're trying to keep this fire burning
but neither of us said a word when the oven broke
or when dinner caught fire
or when we ate off of kitchen chairs in my new apartment
because no matter how many times we enter furniture stores
there is still something missing
when we walk through our front door
it's so hard to make this a home
when your wallet is empty
but part of me wants to believe
when i look at my shiny tv
that somewhere down the line i'll be able to afford it
somewhere down the line we can love each other
even with missing tables
our foundation will be stronger than that
i don't want to look at a door and see you leaving
i don't want to mourn a loss i haven't known
despite being a body covered in kisses
that look like exit wounds
i am painfully aware that nothing ever stays

smoke-tinted light

i wait for you to kiss ruins into my body
every time i look into a mirror
i am forced to forget how to find myself
an abandoned city should never have your lover's eyes
you brim me with memories
until i am on my knees
begging to be spared
i'm just a little scared
of loving you in front
of crumbling monuments
with our stone-faced forefathers
judging us for the way we
love behind closed doors
and i want you to know
that when i look anywhere
but in your eyes
i am looking at your shadow
i am turning on all the lights
so it doesn't disappear
and i'm only afraid of the dark
because i can't tell if you're still here
you and i shed leaves
in the middle of summer
you and i might leave
before we fall for one another
we will hash out our love in court
a custody battle between the parts of
ourselves we left behind
i'll hate the way i still know your favourite colour
you'll always know my eyes are like my mother's
i can't forget the way i just became old news
and i've learned the more i love you
the more i start to bruise
i love you like a hit-and-run
i'll leave a letter under your windshield wiper
and you'll never see me again
i apologize for not knowing how to just be your friend
for kissing you on the mouth

when i should've kissed your cheek instead
for reaching out to hold you every time in bed
i might've ruined you
me
us
this love had a deadline and i kept breaking the clocks
the key didn't fit so we kept changing the locks
we couldn't afford a dresser
so we loved out of an overflowing box
my darling
i saw our future in my dreams
when you were asleep next to me
the ruins on my skin are still here
the lights are blinding
and your shadow has disappeared

fourth of july

how did i get these burn marks on my hands?
well—he told me when he was high
that fireworks have caution signs
because the people who invented them
don't want us to touch the stars
maybe it was the look on his face
or the fact that i wanted to believe
every word from his mouth
but i felt he was right
and when the fireworks left nothing behind but scar tissue
i still couldn't say he was wrong
everything that's beautiful hurts
you just can't see it until the sparks die out
you can't see it until they admit you to a hospital
at three in the morning
and he's too delirious to be your emergency contact
he's tripping over my mother's phone number
there's a gurney against the white walls with his name on it
i learned that week when your skin is laced with charcoal
they rub it off until you see bone
until you see nothing but red and white and blue
his voice calling from outside throbs in your head
this is the third time they've kicked him out of your hospital bed
he doesn't want to leave your side but he's tired
he's been wearing yesterday's clothes for eight days straight
and your family keeps wondering why he cares so much
i tell them he's a great friend and i'm only half-lying
he tells me, when everyone is asleep except for us
that he feels guilty about the fireworks
and i don't tell him
that it's nothing
the burn feels exactly like
the way he loves me

my heart just split in two

they say it's detrimental to fall in love
with someone who hurts you
but sometimes i don't mind
especially when i'm listening to 505
by the arctic monkeys
your hands are twisted around my throat
and my friends tell me they don't know me anymore
i guess that's true
and it's all down to you
and your stupid skinny jeans
and bruises raised round the edges like tattoos

i'll say it tonight
i'll say it again
i'll say that i love you with a gun to my head
but the worst part is
i can't say i didn't know any better
the worst part is
you're the one who pulled the trigger

mri love you

i need to find a new metaphor
stop comparing you
to the ocean and outer space
stop comparing you
to house fires and sinking ships
stop comparing you to
every beautiful thing i've
ever been afraid of
even though what i'm trying to say is
i love you so much
it scares me
because
i don't know if you found me
slumped over a half-eaten pizza
and a bottle of extra-strength painkillers
or if you found me
hunched over my laptop working on a thesis
that didn't sound so ridiculous
but i've been trying to kick a nicotine addiction
because it hit me
right in the ribs
when i first met you
and i haven't been breathing properly since
i never wanted to love you between
50-thread-count hospital sheets
but according to my blood pressure monitor these
headaches and you are playing tug-of-war over
who makes my heart beat faster
and it's turning my body into a disaster
and i hope you win
because you make me feel like i can dive into the deep end
even though i can't swim i want to take the risk
i want to love you like
the wall clock in my new basement apartment isn't too loud
like i'm not thinking about how
we're already buried underground when i look at the ceiling
like this place is big enough for both of us
and you stop calling yourself an insomniac

whenever you lie down beside me
we look at the patterns behind our eyelids
and pretend they're stars
and you hold onto my anchor hands
and i hold onto your ship body
and i still love you in mixed-up metaphors
except i'm not scared anymore
because you're sleeping right next to me and
you've never looked so peaceful

the kiss

count my teeth with your tongue
just do it slowly
fall in love with each calcium deposit
until you can't taste anything but me
resting gently in your gums
until they go novocaine numb
and you swallow my breath down
it makes you realize how long you've been drowning
and your mouth stays latched to mine
like it will kill you to stop
inhaling the air from between my lips
this is too intense
to just be a kiss

goldie

to the boy with a me-shaped hole in his chest
and a laugh that sounds like needle on vinyl
i just want to apologize
for diving in too fast
i was trying to feel what you did
every day brings me closer
because tears don't come easily anymore
so when i cry, it means something
it means "stay" and "please don't go"
and "this isn't fair"
why aren't we allowed to grow old
why aren't we allowed to feel the sun kiss our bodies
why does every crack of lightning snap us in two
the weather is vicious to us
every forecast will ruin us in varying degrees
to the boy with a me-shaped hole in his chest
and a cough that makes me check the sink for blood
i apologize for making things about me again
i just wanted to buy more time
i shattered every clock in this goddamn apartment
but you still withered away
daylight savings couldn't save you
and the sun stopped shining too early anyway
you're still dying and that kills me
so, even if it's for a short time,
stay, please don't go,
this isn't fair
i know
to the boy with a me-shaped hole in his chest
that doesn't look anything like me
you keep listening to needles on vinyl to drown
out the sound of coughs that spatter red wine
all over the porcelain sink
to the boy with the hole in his chest
caused by a needle on vinyl
and a hacking, bloodstained cough
i didn't create that hole
but i wish i could make you whole

birthday balloons

i need to stop holding your hand like
i'm holding onto a helium balloon
trying to stop it from floating away
i need you to stay here with me
even if you're not supposed to
i don't care about the laws of gravity
when you're standing right next to me
and your head is up there with someone else
it won't come down
i can't bear to love all by myself
you need to give me something other than
this silence
music that thrums through your body like
blood
or like i used to
i can feel us drifting apart like
this car accidentally hit reverse instead of drive
and you backed into a stupid girl
with a heart too big for her body
and galaxies in her eyes
holding up a sign saying "for sale"
but all you wanted to do was rent
i love you but you never unpacked your shit
you were always so sure that you would leave
you leave the house key jammed inside the lock
for anyone to enter
i try hiding it under the doormat
but you always find it
and put it back
i spent so much time with my heart on the fence
that it got scratched up in all the wrong places
and the marks look a lot like your name
this dumb game we play when your hands hover over mine
this isn't theatre but we keep forgetting our lines
i just want to tell you that i've been here this whole time
trying to convince you that it's okay
if you want to give this thing a try
but right now i'm convinced you're going to make me cry

i just want you to kiss me like my mouth can erase
every horrible thing you've ever endured
like my mouth is the remedy
like my mouth is the answer
but neither of us is asking the right question
there's something in your eyes when you look at me that
screams "yes" or "maybe"
but then again i see my reflection when i look into them
so it could just be me
getting ahead of myself again
trying to create the grey area between lover and friend
we never really fit into labels before
so all we do is wear them
pet names roll off your tongue
like honey
i love it when you call me that
i love it when you call me
stay with me even if it's just to fall asleep
to the sound of my voice
i won't put you on hold
i can keep letting go of your hand
but those helium balloons you let go of
always show up in your yard months later
ripped and stained
so which one of us can carry the blame
i'll carry you across the world if that's what it takes
to tell you that i don't care if we're different
when our souls are the same
what i'm trying to say is
maybe it's safer if i just
hold your hand

communion

dear lord
please accept these words as my sacrifice
my mouth is dry
i am spent
i have nothing else to give you because i have spent
all my love on someone else
he has broken me, lord
and i'm on my knees begging you to fix me
i know we haven't talked in a while
but he's not around and i feel kind of lonely
i keep having that fever dream
the one where i'm looking through a kaleidoscope
at myself and she's angry
angry that i brushed my teeth with whitening toothpaste
until i had a blood-soaked mouth and bruised gums
that white never reached the stain in me
no matter how hard i scrubbed
every song i listen to sounds like the death march
i can't put it on pause
i can't turn it off
i see the faces of my dead friends in the mirror
i see the faces of my dead relatives in the mirror
i see my lover's face in the mirror
and i don't want to acknowledge what that means
my lord i am writing to you in poetry because
i cannot find another way to say that i am scared
i do not know how else to make it beautiful
god, he looks like a sunrise
up north in the winter
you're not sure he'll come back
he traces suicide letters onto the skin of my back
i don't know if he'll make it home to dinner
i keep hearing the death march when he moves towards me
i think our wedding will need a pyre
please take this poem, my lord,
please take this pain
i'm sorry i can't do this anymore
i don't know if he'll make it to twenty-four

lord i am not strong enough to hold on to his grief
there's no room in my apartment to put it down
my lord i am spent
because i spent
all my love on someone else
i'm begging you, please
sing to me,
a hymn that will restore my belief
a song that won't make my ears bleed—
are you there god?
why does your song sound like the death march?

STAGE III: BREAKING

"Every man is broken in some way. The question isn't if loving him is worth the pain; the question is, will he use it as an excuse to hurt you?"
—Zaynab Al-kari

Do you want to know what I see when I close my eyes?

I see the rage in yours.

I see your hands curled into fists. I see you breaking the desk in our living room, bringing my camera equipment crashing to the floor. I plug my ears against the noise. I blast music through my headphones so I don't have to hear your venomous voice spitting out threats.

I always told my friends I didn't leave because:

I am afraid of hurting you.
I am afraid of your temper.
I am afraid of losing you.
I am afraid of your wrath.
I am afraid of missing you.
I am afraid of you yelling.

I am afraid.
Of you.

night light

i want to let you know i've started sleeping
with the door locked and the lights off
the one thing that scares me more than the dark is you
every time i close my eyes i see your hands on my thighs
i see your face bathed in the glow of a sunrise
i see you lie
all you did was lie
next to me
i would tell you i love you and you'd pretend to be asleep
i'd see your fingers clench around our sheets
i know i loved you enough for both of us
so you never needed to love me
you just needed a place to sleep, eat, and get that release
you needed someone to love you unconditionally
and i did
i regret it every day
i flinch whenever my phone rings
i jump at the jingling of keys
i ache at the thought of letting you in
i kept playing musical chairs with your heart
and you never let me win

hurricane you

i wrote you a letter on the fifteenth brick
at the front of your apartment building
you started leaving from the back door
i want to say i understand how lovers can turn into strangers
but you're looking at me from across the table
and our hands are intertwined
but i can't feel you at all
you promised me forever
with fingers crossed behind your back
i want to know why the last time i saw you
you compared me to a star
and now you look at me like i'm a black hole
you keep reminding me that hurricanes are named after people
i listen to the weather just to hear your name
loving you is like chasing a sunset
i'm two steps away but can never catch up
and i don't want to be reminded
that somehow nothing was enough
i want to exist in a place where you don't
somewhere where i have nothing to lose
because i've learned that words hurt
as much as punches to the mouth
but fuck, both of them still bruise
so let me build myself an empire
an escape doesn't have to be very far
and please let me kiss the galaxies that rest upon your lips
so i can finally taste the stars

garden of eden

the devil loves me in a foreign language
in a way that i don't understand
my heart gathers dust as it sits beneath his shoe
he is made out of alleyways
i was always warned not to enter
the cement starts to combust beneath my feet
as i inhale secondhand smoke
because it kills more quickly
why do i feel like myself when i'm sinning?
i don't mean to write this poem like a suicide letter
it's just that every line is a cry for help
or a sigh of defeat
the tree in my back garden has started
shedding leaves in the middle of spring
i don't understand its rush to die
everything is growing beautifully around it
the warm sun will hit your face if you turn just right
it won't feel so wrong to give yourself to mother nature
she is the only mother that will let you grow
without yanking out your roots
we can still come back from all of this
we can still be lotus flowers
we don't have to be banished from the garden in order to learn
i don't know why we were tricked
into eating forbidden fruit
i don't know why i still search for the taste in your mouth
i think i only love the devil
when he refuses to love me back

hiding

love left our house so long ago
i wouldn't recognize her if
she was standing right in front of me
you trace letters onto my back and
for some reason your fingertips burn
i want to lie and say it's okay
i want to know
how to tell a warm embrace from a slap in the face
that leaves my tear-stained cheeks red on a day
when the sun hides behind the clouds and the birds keep quiet
even they can hear our silence
then you start to yell
and i don't ask myself if i should tell anyone
because you're doing all the talking for me
you hold your bottle and your pride
i hold my tongue and try not to cry
i don't know why love tastes like her mouth on yours
smells like someone else's dior
and looks like curled up fists
the sound of them pounding against
locked doors
and you've got this fire in your eyes
but i'm the only one who got burned
you have nothing left to teach me but you still insist i learn
and now i'm the only one who seems to see the caution signs
i hold them up with bloodied hands that look like cherry wine
and maybe we can press rewind
and i can talk you out of that fifth shot
because in the end i'm left with all the bullet holes
and you're the one who's sane
and i've been on 10 different medications in the past two years
you've diagnosed me as crazy with an inability to please
i don't hear voices though, telling me to hurt myself
if i did, i think they would sound like you

pain is not romantic

when i first started writing poetry,
i kept reading about people meeting
mysterious strangers in empty bookstores
strangers who touched scars and fixed broken parts

since then, i have been waiting in a lonely bookstore
with a cup of coffee in my shaking hands
i have been trying to find answers at the end of cigarettes
and at the bottom of whiskey bottles
someone once told me that if you drink enough whiskey
it tastes like love
but too much blurs your figure and slurs your sentiments

you never found me in a bookstore,
you found me walking home at two a.m.
clutching a bitter cup of tea
you did not kiss my scars, you created your own
you made new broken parts that crumbled like broken bones

no one is going to love you for
your oversized shirt with cigarette ashes deep in the seams
no one is going to love you for
your whiskey-stained teeth or broken dreams
no one is going to find you
drinking coffee in a bookstore, reserved, and
ask what's hiding underneath

we fantasize, and in turn, romanticize, things out of our depth
books aren't the only things people leave
to wither away on a shelf
i was foolish to assume that someone would love me
when i couldn't love myself

misguided

i think the sun set several hours early
because the last time i checked it was still shining
and the birds were telling stories
and i was laughing
and we were okay
but now i'm surrounded by darkness
even the moon has crept behind the clouds
and you've left me holding onto all of this pain
i can't seem to put it down
i was under the false impression
that i beckoned you into my house
but in fact you stood there
on my front porch
as i begged you to come in
without a housewarming gift
your hands still cold
from our toronto weather
you were nothing but the rock
that crashed through my window in the middle of the night
the glass that pierced my skin
you ruined my sleep
you shocked my heart
i thought you were different
and you were
but only in the worst way possible
i thought you were my ticket to heaven
but with you i did nothing but sin
i tried to mould myself into someone you'd love
spat out each word with a little more force
i thought you saw right through me
but the truth is
you didn't see me there at all

stop asking me for directions

take a left on broken-hearted boulevard
go south on memory lane
turn right on forgiveness
it doesn't feel so wrong to say your name
ask for directions when you're wasted
because then it's okay if you get lost
i promise i'll still find you
spend another lazy sunday afternoon
trying to read your thoughts
just by looking into your eyes
oh lord, i could probably swim in them
name them the seven seas or something else ridiculous
to make you hate me
or love me
when you laugh as your fist connects to my jaw
i can't tell the difference between your emotions
body language is still a language
i know how to read it but i don't understand it

smokescreen

it's hard to say the right thing
but you're all i have left
i mistook the smoke blanketing our apartment for fog
one of us had forgotten to turn the stove off
that's how this started
or perhaps it started
when you slept on the couch two weeks prior
or when you told me to stop laughing
and sit still
you used to love the sound of my breathing
said it reassured you
but now it's a nuisance
a reminder that i'm not going anywhere
our foundation breaks
it is not built on anything solid
it is built on empty words
and threats
i'm sorry for the times i carved my initials into your skin
i'm sorry i scratched myself into places where i don't belong
you let me tattoo my name on your chest
and now the scar is infected
a malignant wound that rests on your body
you can't cover the bill to remove it
so you smother it beneath layers of clothing you outgrew
sweaters that look too much like me
another thing in your life
that no longer fits
you force yourself into it
i never wanted to learn how to lose someone
while they're still with me
i don't know why you decided to teach me

mary

keep your hands where i can see them
across the table
away from me
uncross your fingers dear boy
every crevice is a broken promise
these hands that clasp together to send prayers to the almighty
are the same hands that slap this face
it's not blushing if you force it
my cheeks are tinged the colour of roses
you sent to my hospital room
you rose up to shout hymns at me
and i can still hear him yelling over me
amen is what you sing to the heavens
a man mistook my body for his temple
but he's been a sinner lately
thought it would be okay to vandalize
the house of god
you chase down bloody mary's after leaving mary bloody
i caught you red-handed standing
over my body with lips as blue as the sky
i never got the chance to see
you can't wash your bloodstained hands
when remorse is the soap in the medicine cabinet
that you can't seem to reach
while driving with you
i start to leave my seatbelt unbuckled
you kiss me at a hundred-and-ten clicks
you get your license suspended
but still show up at my apartment
with drugstore chocolate and a first aid kit
some booze and a blanket
you try to nurse me back to health
but i flinch at every flick of your wrist
every misplaced stitch
causing damage in places
you don't know how to fix
fist connects to confetti teeth
that shatter upon impact

cutting the insides of your cheeks
mouth connects to bruised
eyes swollen shut, coloured
like the inside of a fresh plum
blade connects to translucent skin
opens up like a waterfall
gun connects to sweat-covered temple
hands shake like brewing tornadoes
trigger pulls back like a boomerang
retracts
and that isn't what i meant when i said
keep your hands where i can see them

sorry

apologies come out of your mouth like
declarations of love
which is to say
they don't
they hide on the tip of your tongue, though
like a forgotten childhood language
the first one you learned to speak
you never knew how to roll your r's
that's probably why it's so hard to say sorry
tell me you're sorry for
not loving me the way you should love me
sorry for letting me believe that you could
sorry for bringing me up just
to let me down
say sorry for being so goddamn ethereal
i was convinced you were made for me
or made to ruin me
everything about you is so inviting
but i was always warned not to enter abandoned warehouses
and you wear houses on your sleeves like tattoos
always trying to offer a home to everyone who looks at you
i was a fool to think i could have been different
that you wouldn't kick me out
i overstayed my welcome
i just want to know when you decided to let me crash
into you but
then stepped out of the way
i lie in a heap of my own debris
my feet can't take me anywhere
but despite that fact
i show up at your doorstep at half past midnight
with my pride in my hands
and my heart in pieces
i've done it again
given you everything and watched you
refuse to give anything back
we spent too much time house hunting
when we should have looked for a home instead

negative balance

my mother didn't know you were
my version of a maxed-out credit card
your words the interest charges i couldn't repay
or replay in my head
she paid every last penny
didn't glance at the balance
while she tried to fix the bond between us that kept slipping
as a result of my loving a thief
she lost six thousand dollars
and her daughter
you were my ponzi scheme
my payday scammer
my kneecap bullet
my online spammer
you took every cent
and left me
senseless
everyone tells me not to run away from my problems
my problems are debt collectors and i'm broke
my problems are loan sharks
and they keep knocking on my door
i have a negative balance in my bank account
and all i want to do is run
you know what happens
when you can't pay debt collectors back
they start with your house
then they burn your assets to the ground
but loan sharks
they start with your family
until they get to you

maybe you should take some advil

i shouldn't have taken a sip of the first man
who told me that i have hangovers for eyes
all filled with regret and
looking like they don't belong in my head
i just thought he'd work like 12-hour aspirin
but the medication never kicked in
especially not when my teeth were being kicked in
i didn't mean to wear eighteen that well
especially not when i was twelve
in the arms of strangers who acted like they knew me
late at night the memories consume me
and leave me shaking,
post-traumatic stress leaves me aching
mistaking red wine for fruit punch
left me knocked out cold
and i wish i could tell you that
these hangovers go away when i close my eyes
i shut the blinds and take everything in the medicine cabinet
but the voices still ring in my head
reminding me that it's stupid to love a girl
everyone kept leaving for dead
i keep trying to love the reflection in the mirror
but she won't look at me anymore
keeps reminding me of the times
i pointed out every imperfection and tried
to rip it away like it didn't belong to both of us
like it didn't belong to the twelve-year-old
girl with the crooked teeth she didn't care about
because she was too busy laughing
the scrawny figure that she didn't worry too much about
growing into
and her heart was always twenty sizes too big
so she started losing that weight each birthday
until her heart got a little too small for her body
until she turned ice cold and couldn't love anymore
maybe she's got hangovers for eyes
because you kept sliding over drinks
someone should've told her that

she never owed you shit
not a crooked-toothed smile
or a scrawny has-been figure
or a plea
or a memory
but you took it anyway

2%

i have nothing left to say about you
your face looks like it belongs on the back of a milk carton
i turn the picture around just so i don't have to look at it
the guilt makes me choke on my breakfast
i sit at the kitchen table across from a ghost that has your eyes
and you don't smile when i hold your hand anymore
i tried to get drunk
on the last bit of vodka i had left in the cabinet
i was trying to forget you but
you were right there
the memory of you buffering in front of me
you turned this house into a green screen
people talk about love filling you to the brim of your mouth
but love empties me out
till i'm splattered all over the new porcelain tiles
and you're crying over spilt milk
cleaning up the mess
you see your reflection in the puddles on the floor
and i want you to know
that it's alright if you look like a picture
on the back of a half-empty carton
i will miss you until i run out of milk

our favourite date spot is the er

you siphoned your way into my soul like a foreign substance
contaminated with the blood of all your exes
hoping my love would be the right one to gamble with
all the while ignoring the odds
maybe the third time isn't a charm
but you seemed so charming looking at me the way you did
i forgot that
blood transfusions can cause untreatable illnesses
when the blood isn't tested
and you should never share needles
with anyone no matter how much you love them
you don't know where their dna has been
i admit sometimes i think the radiation took hold of my brain
your name slams against the marrow of my skull
and this is my sixth mri since i met you
they can't seem to figure out the reason for these chronic head-
aches
and i want to tell them:
you're sitting in the waiting room
with your hands crossed in your lap
and you keep checking the time
itching to get home to someone else
but i don't say anything
because stress manifests itself in bacteria
that breaks down your immune system
and mine was never that strong to begin with but
every time i think about you i start to cough
my temperature climbs
and our memories erupt from my mouth
until i'm left with the aftertaste of rust
and everything i say makes you flinch
every time i say i love you
you call an ambulance
the headaches start to get to you as well
i don't check the time while i'm waiting for your results
in a white room that smells too much like your favourite drink
because the only person i'd want to go home to is you
and i'm sorry i loved you in a way that's incurable

i just wanted to see if my heart would stop
when you kissed me
but i didn't realize you wouldn't pick up the defibrillator

ghosts

i cannot believe how many days i spent
plucking petals off of flowers,
trying to see if you loved me
only to realize i was ripping something apart
to keep myself whole
and today i tried to fit the mould
of a girl you once loved
that self-deprecating waif with long hair
and bags under her eyes
that you loved to romanticize
because it made you look like a hero
why did we think it was beautiful
to smoke menthols and listen to other poets on stage
talk about all the ones they've lost
a bunch of aching souls sitting in a lonely bar
you held my hand beneath the table
as if you knew i'd be up there one day
i think the ghosts have given up on us
they've retreated, they have nothing left to haunt
i heard them say
"my god, the living are more soulless, than the ones already dead."
i promise them this pain is only in my head
hoping they won't hear my heart breaking in my chest
and i know you're living your life now
pretending that i never existed
i admit, sometimes i don't think i ever did
i promise i'll stop writing poems
if you stop sending me letters
that end with you saying you love me
but not enough to stay

mutt

late at night when my soul
dislocates from my body i get scared
the dogs in my
neighbourhood
smell the fear
and begin to howl
i join them
chasing down
guttural groans
with over-the-counter
cough medicine
the non-drowsy kind
because i haven't slept like
a baby since '95
and i'm not about to start now
i listen to the sound of my heart
like it's a lullaby
but the song never seems to end
as much as i press stop
morning never comes
quickly enough
i wake before my alarm
and dress up only to
dress down
these high-waisted jeans
always go to waste
they look better on the bed
of a woman you don't
intend to wed
falling in love is a chore
a bore
love, the proverbial whore
always going door to
door
searching for someone
new to feast on
looking for a girl
who can't tell stories

and laughs a lot
you've found me
i wear my heart on my wrist
like a broken watch
like an accessory
after the fact
that i gave too much of
myself away
too quickly
i'm afraid to try again
i make enemies of my friends
and lock them out after
letting them in
i pay a fixed mortgage
on a house of ruins
i love roses only because
they're the colour of blood
and that looks like
everything i've ever been
afraid of
my headboard
masquerades as a
gravestone
and the fingernail scratches
on its wooden surface
read like eulogies
my bed bugs me
it leaves me feeling
sick, uneasy
kind of queasy
i want to fix it but
my room reeks of mistakes
and lavender
and failure
and whatever smell the dogs keep howling at

one-trick lover

i think i'm in love with the way you love her
you scratch your nails into her back
like angry hieroglyphs
i know it sounds bad
but hear me out
the marks read like poetry
blood-red ink spattered against your bedroom floor
and she is wearing your favourite shirt, no pants
while she sleeps in your arms
you love her like running laps around the track
like the timer is a bomb about to explode in your eardrums
the sound of her voice telling you you fucked up
that if you ran a little faster you could've saved her
from taking the shotgun at the beginning of the race
and putting it right in her mouth
lighting it up like a cigarette
and smoking her own body
i mean c'mon,
you started telling her that death could be beautiful
why are you so surprised that she believed you
why are you so surprised that she tattooed her body with razors
that she branded herself with matches
that her smile never matched the desperation in her eyes
her mouth pulled you in
but everything else was begging you to look away
it's okay that you could only love her like a magic trick
saw her in half
and make her disappear
but she never comes back
and you stand there like an idiot
the spotlight strips you of your dignity
the curtain doesn't close
and you should have refused
the first time she started taking off her clothes
shouldn't have called it love
when you etched poetry into her skin
i know you think you're innocent
and i get that but

if you ever want to know why
she extended her disappearing act
just look beneath your fingernails

skin upon skin upon skin

i tried to let go of you
my fingernail marks stayed branded into your skin
like a painful reminder
every time you look at your body
you feel hot coal
or iron
or me
every hickey was filled with venom
but you kept tossing out the antidote
i was only trying to help you
i held you
and cracked your ribs
into matches
you use them to light your cigarette teeth
you said you'll forget me
but have you looked at your skin
my name is creased into every crevice
your body betrays you
every time you see it

rose-coloured lenses

i leave my rose-coloured lenses hidden
in an old messenger bag
when i look at grey skies i see colour instead
am i lying to myself when i see something dark
as different shades of red?
is it wrong that i can only look into your eyes
when i'm wearing them?
i need to see a distorted version of you
i can't meet your gaze with a clear vision
it frightens me too much
to leave my insecurities at the door
to see you in a way i haven't seen anyone before
but that's what you keep telling me to do
i leave my past on the porch beside my shoes
this isn't love but that's all we're trying to prove
to each other without saying it
but i kind of want to
not in the way that we're both afraid of
i wanted to apologize
for the times your dad told you to just be a man
for the times we crossed the street and i almost held your hand
for the time i swallowed the truth and it burned going down
it's painful to admit that we look for sanctuaries in a ghost town
it's even more painful to admit that solitude is found
in the spaces between my fingers
i just need to fill them with something
maybe a drink or cigarettes or
you
or anything
after a while it all feels the same
after a while even lenses start to fade
we broke those frames in a fit of rage
i asked you who you love and you couldn't say my name
i don't want to watch this thing go to waste
we're made of atoms and
matter changes states when it's heated or cooled
but if things get too heated let's change states
like it doesn't even matter

i'll meet you in the middle of the border
when we get over the fact
that you were cold to me last time we spoke
told me with your eyes that
you didn't want to see me anymore
i just want you to know
if you can't look at me like you used to
you can always borrow
my rose-coloured lenses

crisis

it starts with snow
in the middle of july
i'm walking with you
but i'm ten steps behind

it is a normal tuesday afternoon
save for the fact that you
have bleeding gashes on your arms
we can't find the first aid kit

we set a date to sit down
and write our suicide letters
you take out your notebook
you start without me

the streetcar lets us off
in front of a cathedral
we sit outside
as if there's something stopping us from going in

people like you and me
enter churches
because we got lost on our way
to the mausoleum

snow-covered summers

i remember it now
we couldn't find the corkscrew for the cheap wine
you left hidden in my dresser
so we decided to taste each other's mouths instead
that was fine with me
teeth break under foreign tongues far too easily
and you dodge bullets every time we have a conversation
because you aren't feeling this anymore
you don't want to talk like you used to
i remember it now
because we're the same, aren't we
i wear past lovers in pastel-coloured
turtleneck sweaters in the middle of summer
everyone looks at me like
babygirl you're crazy
but i'm just
so cold
i remember it now
you're peeling out of my driveway
not looking in the rearview mirror at my face
and it's such a disgrace to love you this way
i am chewing and spitting out terms of endearment
and i love you like
flame to unopened letters
love you like
tequila to destroyed liver
love you like
washing machine to dry clean only
love you like
this
your hand a closed fist around my heart
squeezing tightly
till you choke my love's name out of my lungs
so all i'm left with is a hacking cough
and cigarette ash in my hair
and your hands are everywhere
searching my body for a crevice to hide in
you don't find anything so

you start cutting me open
out in the open
under cocaine-white clouds that start pouring
and my heart is beating a million miles a minute
because i'm finally feeling something
and goddamn it, i miss it
it sounds so beautiful when i
rip myself apart
in a way that only you know how to
because
i remember it now
and i wish that i didn't

STAGE IV: LEAVING

"The centre of every poem is this:
I have loved you. I have had to deal with that."
— Salma Deera, *Letters from Medea*

I can tell by the way you look at me that I will never hear an apology from you. I can tell you'd never give me the satisfaction.

My therapist tells me that you probably don't have the ability to feel emotions the way normal people do, and that's only confirmed when I remember you telling me you don't know if you ever loved me; you don't know if any of it was real.

I ignored the last text message you ever sent me, and I think it bruised your ego because you look at me the way I should be looking at you.

I gaslight myself, remembering your hand cupped around my cheek, remember you saying you'll never leave. I remember the night I lost my vision, and everything went black, you turned off all the lights so neither of us could see. That's love, right? You kept my spare inhaler in your bag; you rushed to get it after every asthma attack. I could never breathe right when I was near you.

You acted so in love with me.
You acted so in love with me.
You acted so in love with me.

You acted.

I'd give you an Emmy for that.

please take off your shoes

i have come to the realization that i was wrong
to love you the way i did
so focused on kissing your bright red lips
i didn't taste the blood
i loved you the way the ocean loves the sand
i always pull away at the last second
but still, i come back
we ruined the welcome home mat
it only says come home now
well, won't you come home?
see there was an alert on the news last night
saying that there's a criminal running loose
breaking into places and
i still left the door open
but i don't know if i did that for you
or because i want to feel a pain
that i can pretend i deserve
and close my eyes and see your face burnt into my skull
i'd tattoo this wedding ring onto my skin
if it meant i was never tempted to take it off
every person after is just another version of you
like when you try to find that one poem you read ten years ago
and have to read a bunch of other ones about the same subject
they're only echoes of what you really want
you try to pretend it's the right poem or right person
but all it is is a replacement for the aching
all it is is rehearsed loving
rehearsed touching
rehearsed everything
reverse
step back
i think i'm going to get
rid of the welcome mat

wedding bells are deafening

hey
i don't love you
your smile just looks like an emergency exit sign
and i've had one foot out the door for a while
maybe i should dial this back
it's okay if you leave but just know
i'll probably beat you to it
i don't care if this is the wedding dress i've always wanted
the gazebo lights can't make up for the missing spark in my eyes
hey
i don't love you
a storm came down at my bridal shower
i should've known
i'm not feeling anything for you the
lightening just happened to strike me
you consummated our marriage
when you fucked me
over
hey
i don't love you
i put hearts over the i's in my name on the divorce papers
i asked to keep part of myself in the prenuptial agreement
but you just took it anyway
it wasn't fair game
you ignore the legalities so
excuse me if i ignore the formalities
when i tell you
to put this ring where the sun don't shine
and if that happens to be directly over our apartment
so be it
i always liked the clouds anyway
they also have commitment issues
disappearing every chance they get but
they always come back
you're no good at that

hey
i don't love you
i couldn't hear the wedding bells
over the ringing in my ears
i couldn't meet your eyes
when mine filled with tears
i wore this garter like a noose
i caught the bouquet
hey
i don't love you
so let's raise a toast to every delusional person who does
all our guests who were always jealous of us
to all the people who assumed forever would be enough
to the dj who accidentally played a break-up song during our
first dance
i hate him for jinxing a thing that never even stood a chance
hey
i don't love you
i love the idea of starting somewhere new
with a picket fence and an intimate friend
a utopia where i create the rules
i don't know why this daydream always seems to include you
hey
i don't love you
you always had your wedding cake and ate it too
chocolate and vanilla don't really taste that great together
and our guests threw out their party favours
so do me a favour and tell the venue we want our security de-
posit back
i mistook commitment for a life hack
i should have chosen vegas
everyone makes mistakes there but i chose the city
that knows me too well
hey
i don't love you
i don't know why i said yes
this wasn't a shotgun wedding
but this wedding has left me with a shotgun between my eyes
i fell for the groom who
got over the bride

hey
i don't love you
you couldn't look at me when you read your vows
in sickness and in health
made me feel sick
for better or for worse
and things only got worse
hey
i don't love you
except for when
i do

basement blues

i have never known a love that didn't taste like rust
so when your tongue broke each tooth in my mouth
and blackberry wine spilled from my gums
i wiped the floor with stars in my eyes
mistook pain for passion
because they looked so similar when it came to us
i used to beg for every touch like a dog at the dinner table
i was content with the scraps
let you leave far too often for my liking
because if you didn't leave, how would you come back?
i don't want to look at my bed, my house
i don't want to look at what used to be ours
i don't want to spend hours in a pile of dirty laundry
trying to find one of your socks
so i have an excuse to tell you you forgot something here
and maybe after a few months of this you'll realize
what you forgot was me

co-dependence

i don't think i can save you anymore
i didn't pull the plug out of the bathtub
when i noticed you'd fallen asleep
i was just a little tired
from carving our names into the porcelain
of the toilet seat
you woke up choking for air
with a smile playing on the edges of your lips
death is the closest emotion you can ever link to happiness
i don't think i can save you anymore
i deleted the alarm off my phone that
reminds you to take your prozac
i watch you throw each pill down the sink in the bathroom
i smile when you open your mouth to show me the pill is gone
we keep swallowing each other's lies instead of medication
and wondering why neither of us can get better
you write reminders to yourself on
my unopened hospital letters
before we go to bed
reminders to yourself not to lose your fucking head
and sometimes you'll clench your fists before you touch me
pull my hair a little harder than you meant to
and i'll still go to you for a kiss
sometimes i don't recognize the taste of my lover's lips
sometimes you'll put parts of yourself on the grocery list
we keep breaking one another for the sole purpose
of seeing which parts of each other fit
until your hands clench, teeth grit
you've got my pent-up anger
and i've got your sarcastic wit
we hate each other more than we love each other
but you're the one drug i can't seem to quit
i look for you in the empty medicine cabinet
on the wrong side of the bed
whenever i'm not filled with you
i'm filled with this sick sense of dread
i just need another hit of you
until the monster in me has been fed

i wish i believed the people who told me
that addiction is all in your head

predictions

i could say i love you like this:
i learned from you how to wield a pen like a gun
and shoot all my sorrows onto fresh paper
with blood-red ink soaking the page
i dot my i's with bullet holes
but i should be honest
and write you a love poem that isn't so lovely
because you break me open
you and all your incandescent glory
when you meet my gaze from across the table
with a laugh that looks like
someone lit matches behind your eyes
i love you but
your vinyl heart spins out of control and away from me
your wiry frame and defeated gaze are hauntingly beautiful
when you fall asleep next to me but you're not touching me
because you're scared of what i think this means
and sometimes you're so fucking mean
because you love me too
but only when it's convenient
you run out of gas right when you get to my street
and you can't find anywhere else to stay
you spend the night and i wake up beside you
with my hands balled up like fists throwing punches
because you were right when you said that
the one thing i know how to do best is love an addict
all i do is give and all they do is take and take and take
until there is nothing left to take anymore
but you start clawing at my skin anyway
until my bones start to crumble underneath your nails
look at this carcass and feel some sort of remorse
for what you've done
your selfishness has won
i'm nothing but a pit stop for you on your road to self-discovery
nothing more than a trophy on the shelf
you'll let me gather dust and then replace me with someone else
because all i know how to do is fix
and all you need is a fix

and i guess the definition got lost between us
when i reached out to hug you
and you thought i was asking for a kiss
i try to hit your heart with a bullseye
but i always seem to miss
listen
i don't want to love you like this
or at all
poems about you used to fall from my mouth
but you've emptied me out
what good are my salty tear raindrops
when my heart is in a drought
what good is your incandescent glory
if every touch leaves me with scorched fingertips
i hate to see myself like this
but what's the point of leaving to make a point
when i never leave you anything to miss
i just need to stop branding your name onto my wrists
i need to stop looking at my house
like it's the result of a continental drift
in the midst of all our breaking and separating
i kept thinking it was bliss
i keep finding your things hidden
all over my house like fossils
where they don't belong anymore
and i keep finding bits of you stuck in my skin like glass
because there is no beautiful way to say that
loving you fucking hurts
so maybe i'll leave
in hopes that every copy of me you try to find is still rough
because you should've realized that you had the sun
so why did you want every other damn star?
and why wasn't i ever enough?

forever, and other lies

you have swallowed the universe
and i can see galaxies in your eyes
i don't think i ever stood a chance,
did i?
i'm sorry if i led you towards
broken bridges
and asked you to cross them for me
i'm sorry for expecting you to say no
i'm sorry for asking you to push me on
a rusted swing set
the weight of my regrets
made it break
and it's not your fault; it's my mistake
i'm sorry for asking you to dance
and then stepping on your feet
i've never known how to be elegant
(can you find it in yourself to teach me?)
it's hard for me to talk about forever
because whenever someone promised it
it never came true
forever ended in tears and empty apartments
forever ended with you

stars in her eyes

i don't date anymore
the only thing i date is my journal
when i'm writing poems about you
the only thing i date are the cheques
i mail out to you monthly
maybe i'm doing something wrong
because we both know that money's going to your dealer
but it's the only way i can deal
with you being gone
i see the money missing from my account
and i know you're okay
i'm broke these days but i'm still paying the price
of a dwindling fire that we kept trying to reignite
i'll leave the door open and you'll leave at the end of the night
right before things start to get bad
my doctor works from 9-5 but i choose to have my crises at 6
i don't bother calling his cell phone
ohip doesn't cover my phone bill
but the cute guy at the bar can cover my tab if i smile hard
enough
all i have to do is think about you
i'm not going home with anyone else
i don't want to be a one-night stand
i'm too much of a romantic
we'll kiss but we won't hold hands
i'm going to hitchhike to you one day
and either some guy on the side of the road will kill me
or you'll do it when you open your front door
give me back my shit
and tell me you don't want to see me anymore
i mean i get it
but i wish the walls could've warned me
because i swear late at night i hear them talking
and maybe it's the drugs or maybe it's the neighbours or
maybe i just need someone with me in this goddamn house
so i act like i can hear the walls talking
i was born out of flames
i create forest fires on the weekends

in between brief sessions of self-loathing
there is no one who does this better than me
my heart is a crypt
it's where love comes to die
you used to pry my notebook out of my hands
trying to find your name in the pages
all you found was heart-wrenching poetry and
you look confused but all i know how to do
is deal with the inevitable
that's why i leave the door open
that's why you'll walk out each time

cul-de-sac

my rib cage is spun out of the phrase
"please don't go"
my heart hits it every time it beats
like it's threatening to escape
is it fate when my hands clasp around my neck?
is it love when i squeeze tightly?
refusing to let go
i'll put on a show and call it
a public display of infection
it's not an illness i just
don't know where to leave my head sometimes
it always comes with me
taking up too much room
like an elephant
my problems follow me around like my shadow
but when the lights turn off they only get bigger
i keep ripping apart the mixtapes i made you
because nostalgia hurts more than it heals
mistakes these bruises for hickeys
and kissing cruel boys led me to realize that
they don't tease you because they like you
they tease you because you're a little fucked up
and they have nothing better to do
except break your mixtapes
and count your mistakes
you take the contents of the cassette
and string them over your bed
it says
"this heart is a cul-de-sac"
but you keep driving
breaking down signage
and leaving me behind it
you'll understand after spending so much time behind the wheel
that the highway only leads to hell
and you should've never stopped
for the pretty girl at the rest stop
should've never made a town on the side of the road
should've never put a ring on it

should've never lived in your fantasy
people showed up to your wedding dressed for a funeral
and you should've realized then
that every road she led you on was a dead end
that she was lying when she said you'd be better off as friends
and you put down a down payment
on a heart that wasn't vacant
but despite how much she loved you
she just didn't know how to say it
the mixtapes got destroyed in a fit emotion
and the ribbon on the floor reads
"please come back"
you don't

awkward silence

i wanted to start by telling you
i understand why you never met me on that bridge
it never ends well when we talk
and if we don't talk it never ends
we still belong to each other
after months of radio silence
we turn on the radio to fill the silence
you're talking to me
but it's been a while since i've heard your voice
you say my name differently now
like you're speaking a foreign language
my heart can tell you're not from here
listen, i am trying to deal with the distance the best way i can
i gave you your space
so you started acting like we were from separate planets
i think of you so much my skull starts cracking
my ribs burst from the force of my heart pressing against them
you are breaking me from the inside out
i cannot bear to blame you
and tonight i do not want to blame myself
so i blame the cursed thing
that scratched its way into my subconscious
until every dream i painted looked like your portrait
i blame the house we walked past
for being too inviting
we should have never said "one day"
because all it took was one day for me
to try to pin the blame
on every external force that drove us from each other
so i blame mother nature for the parks and lakes
where you kissed me
she could have given me something else to look at
a swan or a tree or anything
other than your face
i blame the leaking faucet for dripping out your name
i blame the pizza guy for keeping all the change
i blame everything until there is nothing else to blame

i keep pointing fingers but this all stays the same
we should've never tattooed expiration dates onto our skin
i should've never resented the way we dove in
i should've never judged you for the way you sin
just because i do it differently
i understand why you never met me on that bridge
it was broken
and i would still have asked you to cross it

you've got mail

i stopped paying for that p.o. box in downtown toronto
i had to take two subways to get to it
i carved the spare key into my skin so i would never lose it
used it to check the mail every day i could
hoping i would find a love letter from you
about missing something other than my mouth
a letter that wasn't so goddamn selfish
tell me i have something else to offer
better yet, forget that i have a p.o. box
find me in your favourite café
that doesn't have a single good review online
the one with the shitty coffee
and broken chairs
and bitchy barista
you always used to take me to
because it had character
your smile cancelled out all its faults
tell me that no letter could convey
everything you want to do and say
and i promise i'll believe you
our love doesn't need a postal code
distance never really meant anything
cigarettes become good for you
after you smoke them this much
they taste like disconnected telephones
sort of comforting, almost
you want to get in your car and make the drive to me
burn every envelope marked "return to sender"
because you know where to find me
and reading your handwriting scribbled onto
dollar store lined paper
makes me read
"i love you"
like
"i miss you"
because you always miss someone more than you love them
and i hope that's what you're trying to say

you always insist on writing in cursive
even though you almost flunked out of the first grade
for forgetting to connect your words
you always had an issue with connection
i realized that after ours went bad
but i forgive all of that
home never had an address
it's always been you
and i don't know how to move out
not with the eviction notice stamped onto my chest
p.o. box rentals were always cheaper than rent
so please send me letters
telling me you miss me
because when you get them back
you'll realize you missed me
but i'll be drinking shitty coffee
on a broken chair
with a bitchy barista
if you ever happen to be in town

piracy

he's still the answer to all my security questions
the one person nobody would guess
how can i say what year i met my lover
when he's not my lover anymore?
these questions are supposed to protect my privacy
every time i log into my bank account
but rob me, take everything, leave me bankrupt
just stop fucking asking me
when i met him,
how long i've loved him,
where he was born
his favourite colour
his mother's maiden name
it hurts too much to answer the questions
about my insignificant other

i wish you'd forget

i still can't forgive
the way you wore your heart on your sleeve
but kept changing shirts
i also can't forgive the fact
that you wanted to know the little things
you spent the night just to figure out
what kind of toothpaste i use
how i take my coffee in the morning
which side of the bed i sleep on
the little things used to be so important
the little things metastasized
into a hollow word that tasted like forever
and colgate
and two milks and two sugars
and the right side of the bed
i can't forgive the fact that
you only loved me when it was convenient
i can't forgive the fact that when i fell for you
i fell face-first into cement
i was chewing up gravel and glass
i couldn't get up
i can't forgive the fact that
you tried to scare me into coming back
i fell into a rabbit hole of our old messages
and now my heart feels heavy
i don't know why alice tried so hard to leave wonderland
i welcome this grief
and it's not that i like the pain
it's just nice to be reminded of a feeling sometimes
everything we started with was poetry
and i can't bring myself to stop writing
i'm just trying to love you
without caring about the consequences

i can't forgive the fact that
the night sky is tainted with your memory
your eyes shone brighter than anything above us
and maybe it's global warming

or pollution
or my eyesight isn't that great
i'm just making excuses to excuse myself
from loving you the way that i do
baby you're like the sun
i know you're burning into my retinas
and destroying my vision
but i just can't look away
i can't forgive the fact that
you taught me how to miss someone when
they're holding your hand and pressing "i love yous"
onto your lips and into the folds of your heart
i can't forgive you
because all you had to do was tell me to stay
and you didn't say a damn thing

since we're being honest

one:
when we look for shapes in the clouds
i always see god flipping me off
i think i deserve it

two:
you never gave me back that promise ring
when promise rings you hang up

three:
we schedule 6 p.m. dinners so we can
sit across from each other and pretend we still give a shit
i mean, i do, but not the way you want me to

four:
you'll lean in for a hug goodbye
but i'll lean in for a kiss
you'll pretend not to notice

five:
i lied when i said i like big cities because
i lose myself in the crowd
big cities make it easier to pretend
you're one of the faces walking past me

six:
i found it ironic how you told me
you kissed someone else on halloween
it scared the fucking crap out of me

seven:
they say it takes twenty-one days to form a habit
i start clawing at my skin like i'm searching
trying to find something underneath it

i still don't know what i'm looking for

eight:
my memories love to betray me
by convincing me that the times before i loved you
meant nothing and maybe that's true

nine:
but maybe it isn't

ten:
i found your vial of coke
hidden behind my old journals
i was only trying to find them
to write about how much i missed you

eleven:
the creak in the floorboards we never fixed
sounds too much like your name
i try not go to home to it

twelve:
i wish you took the fact that your favourite colour is green
and that you sleep on the left side of the bed
with you when you left
i have no use for these things anymore

thirteen:
i don't know if i'm no longer your emergency contact
or if you're okay
i can't tell which is worse

city of love

the french say, “tu me manques”
you are missing from me
and i think that is the perfect way to describe this
empty part of myself
i’d like to think that
i’m doing well without you
et tu, babe?
i hope the emptiness doesn’t hurt as much as it used to
but i also hope it swallows you up like a natural disaster
that’s what love is, isn’t it?
we play russian roulette
and you always draw blanks
then you hand me the gun the final time
we both know what’s going to happen
but i press it to my temple anyway

just blame me

it's the first day of january
and the frostbite on my fingers feels like your touch
i just wanted to come outside to tell you:
i'm sorry
it was my fault
i should have known better
should've never hurt you the way i did
i fucked up
okay, no i didn't but
i can pretend i did if it means you'll come back
i'll take the blame
i'll foot the bill
i'll take care of everything again, sweetheart
i just want you to look at me the way you used to
i want you to kiss me instead of apologizing
the way you did before
i don't want to keep telling everyone
that you and i don't talk anymore
i don't want to see your silhouette
walking out my bedroom door
i know we were late for everything
because i always wanted more
i wasn't finished holding you
i didn't say i love you enough
i don't want to keep realizing that
i didn't get a clean break
all you did was break me
all that loving you did
was make me feel small
so my new year's resolution is
not to love at all

romanticize this pain

please don't wish me the best any more
i keep waiting for you to show up at my door
i give you everything
you still ask for more
my lipstick-stained coffee cups litter
the bedroom floor
the blinds are drawn
and the thought of your mouth throbs against my skull
lips part for me
red like the sea
taste like titanium
and translucency
and regret with a side of
tequila
to kill a girl's inhibitions
i'm sorry i drank so much
of the punch
that it knocked me out cold
i didn't know what to do with my hands
they kept tipping the jug over
and midnight never came
when the clock strikes 12:00 tomorrow we
can pretend it's a new day
and you're not looking at me like you want to destroy me
i will reintroduce myself to you
say my name is baby
and your hands would look lovely around my throat
it's okay if i don't know you anymore
you don't care if i have
crooked teeth and two left feet
you smile at me like
i told you i love you for the first time
and the refrigerator light shining on your cheekbones
is beautiful
i'll pay the electric bill
just to see you like that
all loose and laughing
and lovely

i can't stop thinking about the way
your mouth moves when
you say my name
you say it with force
with bliss
with spite
i look at you with love
and you look at me with grief
it's okay if our love letters are eulogies
we never knew how to love like normal people
and normal people never knew how to love like us

keepsakes

i just want to know you think of me
the way i do of you:
like i'm suffocating
and it's your hands that are
holding my head underwater
i want to know if you still have those pictures
from our trip to montreal
i want to know if you destroyed them
i want to know if you still wear the ring i got you
on your pointer finger
so you can point the blame at me for making this end
i want to know
if you still sleep with your glasses on
if you still have a headache the morning after
miscommunication makes conversation hard
but blocked communication makes it even harder
i try to stay away
but thinking of you reels me back in
i know i want nothing to do with you
i avoid the places you used to frequent
but i look over my shoulder for you anyway
i only want to see you in my daydreams
because that way i can choose the ending
and it doesn't involve you walking out of my life
and into my nightmares
it doesn't involve drowning
and montreal trips that end too soon
you, instead, wear that ring on the third finger
of your left hand
and put your glasses on our nightstand
and hold me close
even though i know you don't want me anymore
i know there are plenty of fish in the sea
but there are a million holes in my net
i refuse to believe you're a memory
so i to force myself to forget
i don't want to remember you saying you hate me
when i hadn't stopped loving you yet

golden girl

my hair smells like cigarettes
your skin is underneath my fingernails
and my mouth tastes like your favourite drink
i had to try the one thing that can make your tongue
scream out
"yes" without it being laced with mine
two in the morning
and it is you
body twisted but open to welcome you
and i wanted to tell you
i've been having withdrawal symptoms
since you withdrew
it's okay to have this conversation
i'm going to fake drunkenness
so you can't hold it against me
but i hope you hold it against me
hold your body against me
god damn, you make me want to bite my lip until it bleeds
and bite your neck until you scream
i want you to come
back
erupt like a volcano and i'll call you pompeii
people will spend eternity
writing about that time you rocked the world
archeologists aren't going to study us
and i honestly don't want them to dig up our remains
because nothing ever remains
the fragments can't explain
everything we ever were
so for now just say my name
take a drag of it
see how it feels in your throat
it's okay if you cough a little
that just means your body
is feeling it too
smoke my name like your lungs are gold
and your body can take this form of debris

there's a reason
my hair smells like cigarettes

salt and vinegar

your love stings the corners of my lips
like extra-salty chips
i stopped having those as midnight snacks
when i realized they made the memories come back
i try to claw my way out of this dreamlike haze
where you're still wrapped around me and
everything is still okay
i try to have a spring cleaning for my mind
throw out the boxes of everything you left behind
i know no bottle of mr clean is gonna take away this mess
because the dirt under your fingernails
is laced with my skin
is laced with sin
laced with whatever we found
underneath the pews of our favourite church
this isn't confessional but i gotta beg for your forgiveness
i didn't love you right
i choked the feeling out of your lungs
when you were already struggling to breathe
i broke your inhaler
made you leave the house for long brisk walks
and by the end of it you couldn't tell
if i was screaming at you or your body was
it's easy to pretend that love is a dead end
when we always avoided main roads
took the more complicated routes to miss traffic
always in a rush to get to an unknown destination
i'm sorry if i pushed you into the deep end
before you learned to swim
i was just trying to see if you knew what it meant to be human
the metaphor was wrong though, you shouldn't dive in
because at the end of the day
my heart is not a public pool that only goes eight feet deep
my heart is an ocean
that will drown you with force
you can't take your tea with salt water
it'll destroy your insides if you try

4:26

it's always four in the morning
when my ring finger starts to feel heavy
when the left side of the bed starts to feel empty
when your phone number looks a lot like
the number of times i had to convince myself
not to call you
just to say
hi
and
i miss you
and i still have weather updates for your city on my phone
i know there was a storm last saturday
i hope you didn't sit through it alone
the thunder frightens you but
lightening reminds you of flash photography
and you were always a sucker for my dslr lenses
you loved how they made everything seem a little more beautiful
and high definition photos of happier times
are my favourite form of nostalgia simply because
you knew how to look ecstatic even when you weren't
i want to call you and tell you that i wrote about you so much
i think i got carpal tunnel
i didn't go to the doctor
so i don't know how to fix it but if you answered
i'd probably tell you that
you could hold my hand and it would cure me
you would shove me and call me a dumbass but
can you please
kiss my mouth and make my mind shut up for a little while
it keeps nagging me about you like
i get it
my head and my heart keep playing this game of tug of war
and my sanity is stuck in the middle
i hope the rope breaks
before i do
and that will probably give me the courage to find you
sitting in your favourite bookstore
the one you probably don't go to anymore

because people change
but i can't seem to
i don't know if i can't let go or if i don't want to
i can't explain that saying your name
is like speaking in my mother tongue it just
sounds right
tastes right
it doesn't have an expiration date
i don't know if we were in love or if love was in us
and we just didn't know where to put it
are we soul mates or did our souls just mate
did our hearts have a one night stand
but make the mistake of calling back?
that's how we got into this predicament
it's divine intervention
we are just puppets on a stage
the strings are too tight around our wrists and ankles
we dance to a tune that's unfamiliar
and i miss you when you're standing right next to me
i love you more at four in the morning
than i do at any other hour
that's probably why the lonely people
should just go to sleep

serial killer

i know you're probably sleeping right now
but i'm going to tell you this anyway
i want this to be the first thing you hear
when you wake up
and part of me hopes that it hurts:
you robbed me of my self-love
ripped it out of every nerve ending
took it with you
i don't know where to find it
you left the door open after this break-and-enter
left my body like a crime scene
every night i wrap myself in caution tape
but still pray you'll come near me
i run to you in a dream state
and it obliterates me
my legs are moving but i'm not going anywhere
you are never there when i wake up
i am never okay with that
i want to know what made you
pull every tooth out of my gums
i haven't smiled since you left
my tongue hasn't said the word "love" in an eternity
it's like you took it out of my mouth
and i didn't notice because it was laced with yours
every body part is buried under your floorboards
but that love, you keep that as your token
proudly displaying it to everyone you see
when i walk past you with my head held down
and you refuse to make eye contact
how do you make murder seem so beautiful?
how did you convince our friends that it was okay?
like all of my injuries were self-inflicted
and i start to believe that
because you warned me not to come too close
but i've never been a good listener
and now that you're gone the ringing in my ears never stops
i don't how to love myself with missing body parts

i don't know how to love myself without you
standing behind me in the mirror
i don't know how to love myself
because i am not myself anymore
i am simply an echo of everything you did to me
i am defined by every missing tooth
defined by always missing you
and i know it sounds like i've given up
but please, do me one last favour as soon as you wake up
help me rip apart your floorboards
i want my body back

95101903R00090

Made in the USA
Columbia, SC
08 May 2018